A POET'S JOURNEY

A POET'S JOURNEY

Bon Voyage

SAM MIRROR

Copyright © 2012 by Sam Mirror

All rights reserved under Win-Win Guru LLC

No part of this book may be reproduced or transmitted in any form or by any means; electronic or mechanical including photocopying, recording or by any means of retrieval systems without Written permission from the publisher.

For Information on reproducing selections from this book, write to

WIN-WIN GURU LLC
WINWINGURU.COM
CONTACT@WINWINGUGU.COM

Library of Congress Cataloging -in- publication data

Sam Mirror 2012
A Poet's Journey- Bon Voyage

Includes index.
ISBN 9780998640006
ISBN: 099864000X

Hikkiri- Henye`

"Great leaders, were once great followers."

Disclaimer

I am a supernatural being on a human experience. I am on an audacious path; an upward spiral. My journey is a phenomenon of miracles and mysteries with occasional whirlwinds of turbulence. Triumphing over challenging circumstances and overcoming disappointment has peeled back a few of life's layers. It has revealed that power, faith and persistence are far greater than the impact of failure. Victory is obtainable, if you believe. Personal success is beyond tangible manifestations and is defined by the heart of the beholder. It is my hope that you find your inner winner and locate the path to personal success. "Although we may fall, we get back up again and again until we walk."

I am a helper and defender of humankind, of those who desire to be happy, fulfilled and willing to help themselves. I am but a child in the eyes of the Most High, diligently seeking truth. What I've retained is but a grain of sand, compared to the vast amount of information available. These poetic expressions are extensions of my love, liberty, joy and hope which stem from the depths of my heart and soul.

Some of the principals mentioned are biblical or have been adopted from great minds and tailored to my lifestyle. Therefore, I make no claims or guarantees.

John 8:32

"And you shall know the truth, and the truth shall make you free."

Acknowledgments

I thank and acknowledge everyone who recognized my vision and supported me. You've accompanied me throughout this journey and serve as a source of strength and encouragement. A special thanks to all who assisted me with this project:

Stephen "ILLFLO" Edwards, my editor, graphic designer and mentors.

I acknowledge my mother, for always believing in me, and my godmother, Pam, for always being a positive influence and supporting me faithfully in my many endeavors.

Thank you, to all of my readers.

Dedication

This is dedicated to every unfinished project and every dream deferred
To every delay and/or excuse that gained temporary victory
You may have won a battle, but I won the war!
To every opposing force and obstacle that I've overcame
This is dedicated to every beast that I've tamed
And enemies conquered
I AM A WINNER!
I have fought and resisted all too long
ALAS! I've conquered through persistence–
This dedication is to every ally of support
To the source:
Thanks for every tool and resource.
Thanks for every morsel of love, gratitude and praise.

Table of Contents

Prologue · xvii

Chapter 1 Love = Patience + Kindness · · · · · · · · · · · · 1
   Ingenious Love · 3
   Blossom · 5
   Dear Notebook and Pen, · 6
   Love Struck · 8
   Bliss · 10
   Knee Deep · 12
   Good Vibes · 13
   The Prototype · 14
   Origins of Love · 15

Chapter 2 Peace + Power = A Sound Mind · · · · · · · · 17
   Conclusion · 19
   Sleeping Giant · 20
   Snow-Balling · 22
   The Beat Goes On · 23

  Things · 25
  Reach for Stars · · · · · · · · · · · · · · · · · 26
  Good Knight · · · · · · · · · · · · · · · · · · · 29

Chapter 3 Patience = Virtue · 31
  Grown-ups · 33
  Journey · 35
  Marathon · 37
  Sleeping Giant 2 · 38

Chapter 4 Persistence × Perseverance = Prosperity · 39
  Mirror Mantra · 41
  Eye Opener · 42
  Sleeping Giant 3 · 44
  The Man · 45
  Good Morning · 47

Chapter 5 Inspiration × Motivation + Dedication = Your Destination · · · · · · · · · · · · · · · · 49
  The Formula to Happiness: 30-Day Challenge · · · 51
  The Love List · 54
  Jumping Through Time · · · · · · · · · · · · · · · · · · 56
  Healthy Habit Exercise: · · · · · · · · · · · · · · · · · · · 57
  Manifestation 101: · 58

Chapter 6 (Potential + Faith) − (Fear + Doubt) = Success · 67
  One and a Possible · 69

  The Air that I Breath · 71
  Journal Entry · 73
  History / Her-Story ·75
  Kat · 77

Chapter 7 Knowledge + Experience = Wisdom · · · 79
  Metamorphosis · 81
  The Cultivated Mind · 83
  The Woods · 85
  Think & Drink · 87
  Infinity · 88
  Sip Slowly · 89

Chapter 8 Divide and Conquer · · · · · · · · · · · · · · · · · 91
  Are You... · 93
  Goldie Locks · 95
  Liar, Liar · 97
  Too Much is Not Enough · · · · · · · · · · · · · · · · · · · 98
  Supermarket · 100

Epilogue ·103

Interactive Workbook ·105
  Personal Love List ·107
  30-Day Challenge ·108
  Thirty Day Challenge Check List · · · · · · · · · · · · ·110
  Journal Entry ·111

About the Author ·123

Prologue

I've often felt like crying my eyes out, yet am not sure why. At times, I noticed that I was pissed off without a cause and ready for war, ready for the jerk who would cut me off in traffic or the new barista that would screw up my latte. Let's just say, I wasn't always a nice person; I think some can relate. I'd alarmingly wake up each morning prepared for the daily battle through New York City's chaotic subway system only to squeeze into an overcrowded train like a canned sardine. Something had to change. I was being drained by my circumstances.   And then, one day, I woke up! That was the day that I decided to change. We assume that something must be wrong when things are not going our way in life. "Only God can fix it," we say. Many people find comfort in thinking that. I find comfort in knowing that the supernatural powers that govern this universe govern my spirit as well and that I have the authority to influence my life and choose the type of experiences I have. I am on a voyage; the good journey. At times I wander seeking adventure, and when I feel myself getting lost along the way, I find solace in helping others. Helping others has taught me a lot. I now know that the feelings I often had was the shedding of an old skin, breaking free of thought processes and patterns that didn't line up with my desires. A new version of myself was emerging;

my desire to become someone with lofty ambitions and grand accomplishments, someone who made a difference in the world, and someone people would aspire to be one day inspired an action. And the journey began. "Who am I?" It took a while for me to understand and every so often I remind myself in order not to forget. I am a supernatural vessel–an instrument here to serve and defend the Kingdom. I've been created for something more. An added yet key ingredient - perhaps I am the spice with the most distinct flavor of all. Or maybe I'm the cherry on top, the one that adds the finishing touch. I am the yeast that raises the cake! And yes, a cake needs time to bake.

Who are you?

I once thought that I was a "people person" when in fact, I feared being alone. Surrounding myself with people was my cover, my disguise to hide the truth. I was not scared, per se, but worried that I had been alone all or most of my life and perhaps my future would be similar. This worry ate me alive. Neighboring myself with people allowed me to avoid the emptiness. Many of us walk around oblivious of our thoughts and feelings, prisoners to our own emotions. The most common way of expressing the emptiness we attempt to avoid, yet in reality consumes us, is complaining. No one wants to listen to a whiner–and whining does serve as one of the symptoms of unhappiness. Recognizing and digging deep to address inner emotions is not always easy but when done properly, one can identify the core root of many problems and arouse solutions. So, instead of whining, I choose poetry as my outlet, spilling my guts out on paper; the judgement free zone. What is your outlet? Using poetry as a way to constructively express my thoughts has enabled me to tap into a care free – creative space which resides within. Our problems and solutions stand right next to one another. Rest assured, for every problem that presents itself a solution will accompany it. If you are like me, then, you are probably someone who believes that life's offerings are far greater than they appear; you are someone who sees the glass as half full verses half empty. It is my hope that this journey inspires your creativity and encourages the pursuit of prosperous living.

Since releasing some of my anxieties on paper, I've learned to appreciate my problems. In the depths of soul searching and confiding in God, I learned to love and embrace life while arising to my destiny. And because I am still human, I too fall short of glory and occasionally fail, but deeming myself a winner, nonetheless, has made me grateful for the discovery of new layers. It is my belief that all things happen for a reason even if the reason is beyond my comprehension. As a result, my paradigm has shifted. I like to call it the "glass is half full vs. half empty" perspective. I choose to live a great life and face my fears by recognizing and confessing them. During life's journey, there will be many stages and phases in which we as people grow through. Our will, determination and faith combined contribute to the outcome of our experiences.

We crawl before walking. We fall down, then get back up again and again until we've actually learned how to walk. If we can envision and believe, then it shall manifest. "Ask, believe, and receive" - that's one of my philosophies. I ask that I'm equipped for the mini battles in which I must undergo.

I ask that each battle that is overcome contributes to my strengths. I ask that the presence of God be with me as well as each of you throughout your journey. I hope that each memoir provides a jewel of wisdom and entertainment for your soul. As you recognize your divine purpose, take time to appreciate life and the uniqueness of each creature that is created.

"Beloved–I pray that you may prosper in all things and be in health–even as your soul prospers."

-3 John 2

Chapter I

Love = Patience + Kindness

Love = Patience + Kindness

Ingenious Love

The love of the creator
Is my fuel
It's my oil
The goal: spiritual success
Love exceeds all
Pressed down, I grind
I'm in tune and intertwined
Life is abundant
Happy and fulfilled
It trickles over and spills
Like beer mugs overflowing
Or mustard seeds sowing
Let it be God's will
I excel with flying colors
Spread joy like butter
Give and receive hand-me-downs of love
From sisters and brothers
Yet of different mothers
One father may we serve
In God we trust!
Therefore, our blessings are well deserved
It is written; it is word
So, I gird my belt with truth

A Poet's Journey: Bon Voyage

And take with me my sword
Dwelling delightfully
Is the eternal reward.

Love = Patience + Kindness

Blossom

A beautiful beginning
A work of nature
As refreshing as a bouquet of blossoming bergamots
I smell your citrus fragrance
The allure to taste you is addictive
It should be flagrant
Amazing are we together
Firmly planted seeds and whether
Attacked by birds or bees
Chocked by thorns
Our harvest grows, faith says
To "grab life by the horns"
Blooming in the winter
In the midst of a perfect storm
Our seeds are planted deep
They shall endure and grow strong
As the sun penetrates the earth
Through the dirt, if it were to scorch our seeds
Love and faith will enable our garden to proceed
It shall blossom and multiply as it achieves
As effortlessly and abundant as a mustard seed

A Poet's Journey: Bon Voyage

Dear Notebook and Pen,

You have served your noble purpose
You have been an unconditional friend
You have helped me heal hearts and mend souls
A reliable tool, you are to me
A navigator through life
The map in which I record
Solutions to one's problems
A host of luxuries, you afford
You've entertained my mind
… Using you, my dear friend
For doodling, sketching and expressing some of my most intimate ideas
Valuable yet venerable thoughts
You, my dear notebook, have experienced firsthand
You were present when I learned to write
Serving as my daily companion
From A, B, C's to 1, 2, 3's
Adding, subtracting, book reports, history papers
Logarithmic equations and thesis papers
You are an excellent platform for any creation
Your blueprints construct the road to happiness

Love = Patience + Kindness

Enabling me to pave a path of success for many trail blazers to come

Thank you.

Love,
Mirror

Love Struck

For love I'd give every worldly possession
I'd walk the longest distance–race the fastest animal
I'd jump for joy
Make you smile–turn your stomach weak
Humble my spirit
And walk meek
For love, I'm taking on all battles…
I'm set and ready
Love is worth defending
In the beginning
Love struck on site
For love I shall live
For love I shall sacrifice
Love's boundless force
Is the reason that hearts beat
For love I'd hop and skip
I'd do somersaults and flips
Part my lips or do a split
Move mountains and rock ships
Whatever it may take to keep love fresh
Filled with spunk and zest
…Willing to do anything
For love
I'll grow; I'll change

Love = Patience + Kindness

To ensure that it remains
In the depths of my soul
Embedded in my bones
Love heals
It makes me whole

Bliss

I could sense that you were near
Closely I listen
A car door slams
Footsteps I hear
Through the curtain I peer
Only to catch a glimpse of your shadow
Cigar smoke rises from cherry wood tobacco
Confidently you enter
Sensual, tall, confident and smart
In my heart there's a spark
Excitement and satisfaction
I know what's about to happen
Heart pounding
I tremble in reaction
Quietly asking myself,
"Is this love or merely a carnal attraction?"
This feeling is overwhelming
"Should I call for help?"
Who would rescue me, and from what?
Nonetheless, in your arms I jump
Pulse racing
I exclaim with elation
Every encounter is bliss
You're my sweet fix

Love = Patience + Kindness

My gum drop, my Hershey Kiss
Like a kid in a candy store
Wanting more and more
You are a variety of delicious treats
My appetite is spoiled when we meet
I have a tooth that's sweet and craves your nectar
…Real love lasts long
Like English toffee;
Soft and sticky
Yet brittle and strong

Knee Deep

In love I've fallen
I can't get up
Knee deep I've landed; my heart is stuck
Out in the sky, bolts of lightning have struck
My destiny fulfilled before my eyes
With intent and luck
My destination; the peak of emotion

In the depth of your eyes
I look within your soul
Your spirit's essence
Discloses your beauty
Behold,
You are the gold
I am
The hopefully, yet, optimistic, miner who's struck!
My destiny fulfilled with intent and luck
I ask for love
Believe in love
I'm willing to give and receive love

Good Vibes

An inspiration
And sensational motivation
From the heart I come
From the vibrations of the drummers' drum
Through birth canals
Miracles are created
I am the opposite of hatred
And as pure as birth
I am as old as dirt
I come in numerous forms
And men's hearts I warm

The Prototype

The love of my life
Completes me
Cares unconditionally
No matter the circumstance
Listens and understands
Loving me for who I am
This letter is for you.
You go to and fro, carefree
All while managing to watch over me
You are omnipresent
So you're never far
Gifting me with your presence
You are my lamp in the dark
Your luminosity twinkles like stars
On those very stars I've wished
And here you are
To my counterpart, fashioned to me
My heart is your lock
You are my key

Origins of Love

Begin
In your heart's center lives a spark
Joy resides
Transmitted energy from the intuitive brain
Echoing in the heart…
It shall endure
Such power shall not be contained
Overflowing and overwhelming
Oozing through pores
Aiming for its desired course
Love travels and spreads

Chapter II

Peace + Power = A Sound Mind

Conclusion

Today is the day I've come to my conclusion
I rid him of my mind;
I shall not suffer from confusion
He's poisoned my mind, body and heart with much illusion
He's covered my ears
Made me deaf
Drawn tears from my eyes
Took all that I had left
I struggled for every breath
FIGHTING! FIGHTING! To avoid death
Emotional that is–not of the flesh
Breaking me down internally
Until soft as mesh
"Hold on!" I said to myself, take it step by step
"He has a part of me now but my soul cannot be kept!"

The lord is my refuge!

Sleeping Giant

I knew you all along
Yet felt as if you were in the depths of the earth's layers or somewhere far away
High above, out of arms reach
Not you;
Brave, claiming victory against all who oppose you
I knew you all along
So close, yet so far;
Close because you reside within in me
Far because even if I dissected myself
I wouldn't find you, nor would I know how to reassemble me
But here you are
Residing in the chromosomes of my DNA
Ready to be awaked
Like a sleeping giant

Hibernate no more!
The season has come for your reign
A time to laugh
A time to cry
A time to plant and to sow

The seeds of my deepest thoughts have been planted in the garden
On good ground

Peace + Power = A Sound Mind

As they sprout
I recognize the beauty of the garden
You have given me all access
You have shown me how to cultivate, maintain its essence
Behold, It is written
This gift is given:
Power to tread upon serpents and scorpions
And over all power of my enemies
Therefore, nothing shall harm me

Snow-Balling

…Life is a ball
And whether big or small
One's focus is their destination

Life is worth living
Is your glass half full or half empty?
Simplicity works

…every learned lesson is a blessing
…seek wise counsel, ask wise questions

Expect the best… and prepare for the best
While others expect the best… and prepare for the worst

… I used to try
… At times, I cry
My tears used to be filled with fears
Now, I cry hearty tears of joy

The Beat Goes On

In the average life time
I beat over two billion times
I never rest, nor do I pause
Like a machine that pumps
I go on and on
BOOM-BOOM-THUMP-THUMP!
As vital as I am to you
I would think you'd consider all that you put me through
Heartaches from old lovers
Or those who you thought were
But I knew better!
Did you listen to me?
The fear in which I felt when opportunity came knocking
You know those things called "obstacles"
All along I knew that they were opportunities
Did you listen to me?
For every tear you've cried
Every battle you've backed down from
For every idea I desired
Yet have not quite manifested
Has caused me to feel unheard and unprotected
It was your mind which introduced you to fear
Listen to me when I speak
72 pumps a minute I beat
I am like a second brain

A Poet's Journey: Bon Voyage

I am the seat of intuition
I shall guide you properly if you listen.
I am responsible for true love, creativity and wisdom
I am the starting point of faith, gratitude and courage
Hear me! Take action when I speak
And forever you'll be encouraged
So please guard me with all diligence
Out of the heart flow the issues of life
Appreciate me!
All I need is to be heard
Over 100,000 beats per day of softly spoken word.
I shall sever as your guide
It's safe to follow your dreams
Live through me and light shall beam
I will guide you straight to your open gate in life
Narrow is the way
And few there are who see the light

Things

Things...Things... Things...

I can't remember things
only songs that singers sing
my mind was polluted with garbage and lots of negative things

Things, things...
Things that bling
Things that ring
Nonsense that distracts the mind from positive things
I'm talking about hindering things that defers dreams
That makes the mind unclean
And think extremely mean.

No more will these illusions
Keep my head in the cloud of confusion
I will control the infusion

I am the problem
I am the solution

Reach for Stars

Growing up, I felt the need to reach for the stars and accomplish something great. I didn't know what that thing would be, but I was determined to find my way in the world. On occasions, I'd become discouraged and my heart would tell me that it couldn't afford to be let down again. I'd remind myself of all the pioneers who had failed thousands of times before achieving victory. I realized that I would have to set my emotions apart from my beliefs because I'd rather be led by faith than fear.

This task wouldn't be easy. How could I could evade reality, escaping from my own thoughts and feelings? I had to make a decision. My mind tried to convince me that I was scared of the possibilities. I had to ask myself: "Does it make sense to want what I don't have or think that I can't have something that I desire?" Ultimately, the price one pays for not perusing his or her purpose, passion or calling is far higher than making a genuine attempt and failing. Though we cringe when we hear the "F" word, no one wants their story to be filled with memories of "what ifs" and buried dreams.

For every time I had hope, I prayed for a miracle. For every miracle I witnessed, I gave praise and glory to the creator for the creation. I am grateful for love, life and abundance even when the path is unclear. In those moments of uncertainty, I meditate in order to access information and guidance from the infinite source that my conscientious mind wouldn't typically conceive. I envision the solution, with expectations that the answer will appear showering me, purging me of all doubt...

If I had a dollar for everything I never knew
For every mistake made
For every concealed thought that went unexpressed
If I had a dollar for every petty human issue I've stressed
A dollar for every sneeze I've blessed
For every time I've stopped to rest
Just think... how much could I have captured had I not slept
How far ahead could I have been... how many extra steps?
What I've learned is that
When I lay me down to sleep
I connect to God and take quantum leaps
I've learned to follow instincts and listen to intuition
That voice that says, "just do it" and "you can make it"
It nudges and assures me that "it can happen," whatever "it" may be
The wise listen and know that the risk is great, but the reward is greater.
It's the risk-reward factor
The motivator of dreams in which we chase after
So I pray that my ears are clean and inclined to truth
That my mind may discern it; know it; accept it and tell it

"And the truth shall set you free."
And when staring into the face of a lie, truth will be there to uncage deceit
I hope for strength, when weak
Nonetheless, I reach.
The exchange is unfiltered positive energy
The risk is great, but the reward is greater

Good Knight

Gazing abroad under dim moonlight
Witnessing the armor of my chivalrous shining knight
Approaching me tall with girth
Confidently walking, planting earth
And suddenly he looks my way
With intention
He's magnetized.
Our universes collide.
Mesmerized by my eyes; instantly
Revelations of our future unfold
He sees the unborn child that I hold
He recalls the choice of engagement rings
He smiles and reminisces on a future that is yet to exist
He then remembers our first kiss
Our first date
The first time I fed him food off of my plate
Smirks and giggles come to mind
Recollecting the day he said, "That girl is mine"
He ponders on late night conversations
That provided mental and spiritual stimulation
Induced by my brain and beauty
He flashes back, from his flash forward
To the day he became hooked
He then says "hello"

As gravity snatches him back to reality
Back to the present moment
As he gaze into my eyes under dim moonlight

Chapter III

Patience = Virtue

Grown-ups

I was taught to be good
But was considered bad
Attractive if you will
I was lied to
"They" said:
"Expect the best, but prepare for the worst"
That never worked
Now, I expect the best, prepare for the best;
Therefore I attract the best
"They" told me to be careful;
Now, I'm careful for nothing
I cast my cares and worries...
What about worries?
What are those?
An illusion of fears
Burdens and cares
When I grow up...
I'm going to be the best version of me that I can be!

Philippians 4:6-7
"Be anxious for nothing, but in everything by prayer and supplication with thanksgiving let your requests be made known unto God. And the peace of God, which

surpasses all understanding, shall keep your hearts and minds through Christ Jesus."

Peter 5:7
Casting all your anxieties on him, because he cares for you.

Journey

Having the map to his heart
Knowing which path leads to success
A journey attempted by a few of the good, yet conquered by the best
While the rest
Fall to the wayside, due to selfish ways and boastful pride
He took steps in stride
Although he tried
It was to no avail
Fearful of trial and error, therefore, he failed
He stayed ashore
His ship never sailed
If to try is to fail
Then one must push and persist
The enemy shall flee if one hast the will to resist
"GO FORWARD! KEEP ON!"
His mind would encourage…
Yet his heart couldn't bear being hurt another time
Disbelief in his potential caused him to draw the line
His heart said, "RETREAT!"
He dared to finish his travels and follow his dreams
Believing that this challenge would lead to defeat
Desiring to finish what he began
He knew that he should
With courage he could

A Poet's Journey: Bon Voyage

Possessing faith, then he would
But lacking these, he didn't
He said farewell to is dreams
"Good bye, good riddance."

Marathon

A discovery was made
On an adventure we went
Passion, love and time was spent
Romance engaged through love signals sent
In subtle voices, emotions were a hint
A feeling of belonging
To a love longing
On our journey
Bridges will be crossed
Challenges faced
Marathons won at a mutual pace
Greatness we'll accomplish
Thanks to my lover, friend and accomplice

Sleeping Giant 2

All along the answers
Were within
Dormant
Like a sleeping giant
Hibernating like the grizzlies during winter seasons
I knew what I was afraid of knowing
I knew that success began the moment disbelief ended
Failure is a part of success
Faith is a part of success
Believing facilitates victory
While the petals of life are falling uncontrollably
Yet, naturally
Gravitating towards earth's dirt
I too shall die one day
And when my flower is dead and gone
Leaving behind the concerns of the world
And abandoning the ignorance which has kept my giant sound asleep
I will fulfill life's cycle
Learn; practice; teach
My seeds are planted deep.
When life resurrects me
I shall return as a vivacious life force
A specimen of beauty, pleasant to the eye
… I will bloom again

Chapter IV

Persistence × Perseverance = Prosperity

Persistence × Perseverance =Prosperity

Mirror Mantra

From the depths of my soul arises a skin-chilling, tear-drawing feeling.
Stemming from a notion
A hunch if you will
"Success follows me"
"Everything that I touch turns to gold"
"I am a magnet of positive energy"
"I am a great…" You fill in the blank
"My testimonies are great"
"I am a beam of light deriving from the almighty source"
"All that I create, shall flourish"
"I illuminate the peaks and valleys of this human experience."

Mantras are a repetition of words, phrases or chants as an incantation of prayer. We are all capable of simply speaking things into existence. We do so by both default and design; intentional and unintentional. It is our God-given power. We are however responsible for what we bring forth by the words we choose and the power invested in us.

Proverbs 18:21
The power of the tongue has life and death, and those who love it will eat its fruit.

Eye Opener

I open my eye; Open my heart
Open my mouth; Love pours out
My whisper snuffs out the hissing
Of talkers who talk and never listen
They sit back wishing
That they were a part of the mission
That they would've opened their minds
And considered my vision
If I could change the world
I'd send everyone a blessing;
Peace of mind, love and learned lessons
I'd ascend above all naysayers
Forgive hateful thoughts and doubts
Of dream slayers
Levitate
Take advantage of how they hesitate
Opportunity knocked; I got my big break
Devoured my pride
Flung my ego aside
I conquered my fear
Never again, shall I second-guess my success
I'm a natural born achiever and faithful believer
Thoughts flood my mind as I compose

Persistence × Perseverance = Prosperity

The journey begins once you hit the road
Take a chance if you hope to strike gold

I open my eyes and my heart
I now have the courage to start

Sleeping Giant 3

On this day I rise
Eyes open wide
Awakening the sleeping giant
Shots fired! Shots fired!
Droplets of rain pour down
In the form of well-drafted contracts
Monogram logo bags and shoes
In the form of hypnotic melodies
Shots fired!
Heavy artillery is being used
Media dispensing bad news
Minimal good news
All tied into fashion's rags
And America's biggest fags…
Ooops! Did I say the 'F' word?

Awake, sleeping giant!
Your minds are being invaded
Robbed and raided

Persistence x Perseverance =Prosperity

The Man

You epitomized what "The Man" means
You were sharp as a whistle and hot like a pistol
Oh, so fresh and so clean
The ideal father and grandparent
Because;
You were "The Man"
A sturdy foundation you built
Keeping your family sound and coherent
We struggle not; not one bit at all
You sustained us well ensuring that we wouldn't fall
Because;
You were "The Man"
Self-confidence you instilled
So let it be God's will
I shall continue to pave the way
A super woman you've raised
I shall save the day
Because;
You were "The Man"
Following your legacy
Walking a noble path
In honor of your name, on your behalf
Of all things that you've conquered, good or bad
Forever your name will ring bells
Your story I shall tell

Your memories are eternally etched in my heart
Because;
You were "The Man"

Dedicated to the most influential man in my life:
My grandfather, Willie Julian Andrews
And to the many good father figures

God bless your souls.

Good Morning

Who arises to contemplate you?
Who awakes to witness your beauty?
To watch the dark creep away like a thief in the night
Only a keen eye will see
Illuminating the sky, you slowly present yourself
A gradual, yet synchronized transition you make
As I diligently watch and patiently wait
Smoothly, you waltz in, and I am awake
Contemplating your beauty
As carpenters construct
Men are loading trucks
Chefs are prepping while city buses lug
People stopping for coffee filled mugs
Simultaneously, an exchange of kisses and hugs
Between parting kids and parents
But, who arises to contemplate your beauty?
To appreciate what's apparent

Chapter V

Inspiration × Motivation + Dedication = Your Destination

Inspiration × Motivation + Dedication = Your Destination

The Formula to Happiness: 30-Day Challenge

I'm sure most of us wish there was an elixir that could make everything in our lives perfect, but the reality is simple: healthy habits create positive change. There is an effective technique that, if committed to for thirty minutes per day, thirty consecutive days, can create massive change in your life. I refer to this as "The Formula to Happiness." I believe that being happy is the beginning of successful living. This challenge began when I decided to do some self-improving. It's like spring cleaning, except I was assessing the different sectors of my life and making a conscientious effort to get rid of old ineffective habits. These improvements consisted of clearly defined goals that aligned with my desires, doing more of the things that I enjoyed and that encouraged me to smile. I ceased all activities that were counter-productive and didn't offer invigorating and stimulating experiences. This combination of activity with consistency was shocking! It proved to be more impactful than I expected. I'm eager to share this formula with the hope that you too will find this technique helpful. Jim Rohn said it best "If you want things to change, you must change."

A Poet's Journey: Bon Voyage

Feel free to try the challenges below. Please be prepare to dedicate thirty minutes per day for thirty consecutive day. Please note, that forgetting or skipping a day is ok – keep going. The steps below can be incorporated into your day as you see fit.

Step one: Journal keeping. Write three things that you're grateful for and express one positive experience that occurred throughout the day. Having the attitude of gratitude is the first step toward true happiness.

Step two : Exercise. Dedicate 10-15 minutes to physical activity. Whether it be a few pushups, stretching or a quick jog, physically disciplining yourself will condition your mind and provide additional energy. Such activities have a positive effect on the body's biochemistry. When I began, I would stretch and do a few push-ups. I could only do about five pushups at max! Seriously, it was sad but true. It made me realize that I needed to build my core strength. So, I set aside time and did a routine of five push-ups every day. I noticed that by day 4, I was able to do about 8-10 push ups. However, it was still a challenge. To make a long story short, by day 20 I was able to do about 50 push ups and could begin seeing results. Through determination, consistency and desire, I successfully increased my overall body strength! In addition, the inches that you'll shed in the process will be appreciated and contribute to your well-being and over all happiness.

Inspiration × Motivation + Dedication = Your Destination

Step three: Meditate & visualize. Dedicate 10 minutes to mental stimulation. Meditation can help reduce stress and maintain clarity. Guided meditations can be found online if you have trouble focusing and calming your mind. I know plenty of people who used guided mediation to remedy this issue when they first began. I prefer to meditate independently since I believe this is my opportunity to listen to God. I use the last two minutes of my meditation time to visualize specific desires. This is the perfect time to use your imagination as if it were a canvas for you to paint the ideal life, since your brain's frequency is between the alpha and theta state of conscientiousness. This is the gateway to the mind's subconscious and infinite intelligence. For example, if you desire a new job or to achieve a specific goal, envision and feel the joy you would feel as if your goal had already been accomplished. Imagine how you'd look, feel and behave; experience it in the now.

Step four: Give praise; be nice and do a random act of kindness. Help someone in need or give a compliment to someone for something you admire about him or her. Kind gestures and uplifting words are edifying to the person who gives and receives the praise.

Will you accept the challenge? Please refer to the tools available in the interactive workbook (page 105-121).

The Love List

- I love my creator and my life
- I love massaging and to be massaged
- I love to laugh
- I love to celebrate
- I love to travel and see new things
- I love to love
- I love to give
- I love to create
- I love providing for my family
- I love flowers
- I love sporty cars
- I love the color green
- I love good energy
- I love a nice hug
- I love happy people
- I love to dance
- I love learning
- I love to help people
- I love you

"Thank you for the love in my heart as well as these lovely things."

Live life to the fullest
Love above all

Inspiration x Motivation + Dedication = Your Destination

Creativity and ingenuity are birthrights
I recall
I lift my voice
I sing
I speak blessings to you all
Therefore
Gifts to you I bring

A visible list of things that you love ensures that you'll keep it at the forefront of your mind. It helps to remind and guide us toward things that are enjoyable in our lives. How often do we get caught up in the structure of life, shortly forgetting our motives and why we work as hard as we do? Circumstances often have the ability to cloud our vision and cause us to forget our "why;" the reasons we live, sacrifice, work and dream, our reasons we succeed or fail. Is your "why" strong enough to make you cry tears of joy or pain? What's your "why?"

Create your personal love list of things, activities, experiences or people that bring joy to your heart and a smile to your face. Be sure to keep this list near you at all times. Read this list out loud daily, followed by a hearty "thank you." This will help you appreciate the experiences that define your life.

Jumping Through Time

While jumping through universes, speaking with my higher self (the better version of who I am), I ask questions such as:

"How do I obtain absolute harmony in my life? How do I manifest the good thoughts and desires of my heart into physical reality? How do I make quantum leaps? How do I remain open to recognizing my mistakes and humbly learning from them? How do I find the place in which is best for me, where there is plenty?"

I could feel my heart race as I was preparing for another leap; I was traveling first class through realms from the comfort of my couch. Projecting forward, I could see visions of who I was to become. In that moment, I was introduced to the real me. My higher self said, "Make a decision, have a healthy obsession with your idea and place your utmost trust in it." My higher self then whispered, "Finish the book." I smiled and said, "Thank you."

Inspiration × Motivation + Dedication = Your Destination

Healthy Habit Exercise:

First things first:

I like to acknowledge the fact that we are the highest forms of God's creations. Hold constructive images of yourself. See yourself the way you desire to be perceived. Envision yourself as a mighty and empowered being. Implement healthy habits in your daily routine such as using the powerful tool we call "imagination." Create a vision of your life that is pleasing to the soul, such as by using your "love list."

- Set goals based on your desires
- Envision yourself accomplishing the goal- See the end result
- Feel the joy in the present moment
- Be realistic: create a plan and strategy towards attaining goals
- Set new goals once you've conquered those that came to pass
- Possess the attitude of gratitude

Manifestation 101:

Manifestation 101 is a combination of practices and healthy habits combined that help bridge the gap between one's desires and present reality. Most folks believe that the gap between some of their deepest desires and reality is further apart than it may actually be. This simple formula along with a few other techniques has been a contributing factor to my many accomplishments and triumphs in life. Some of these ideas and concepts are derived from successors and mentors before me. I have combined several tools, theories, and systems into one simple template. I've had the pleasure of sharing this system and witnessing it work for others, therefore, I trust these concepts to be effective. I make **no** claims that this system will magically perfect your life. I think it's safe to say that no one leads a perfect life; however, there are realistic steps and healthy habits one may implement in order to achieve a desired outcome. Please keep an open mind and do not under estimate the power of simplicity.

Things that are easy to do are equally as easy *NOT* to do. A seeker of growth and change must be willing to do something different, if different results are desired. That being established, I recommend trying this along with my other concepts for about 30 days, though it is said that most habits are created in 21 days. Ready or not, here it is:

Inspiration × Motivation + Dedication = Your Destination

1. Make a decision. Decide what you'd like to accomplish and create the ideal picture or blueprint of your vision; The Universe (Most High/ Source energy/ Creator/ God) is always favorable to those who believe and make their request known. Know that you deserve to be happy, and ask that your desires be fulfilled. You may use your preferred platform to create your blueprint.

   I'm kind of old-fashioned, so I tend to get a pen and paper and jot down a list. When I'm feeling really creative, I'll draw my plan out. Back in 2007 when I began apartment hunting, I decided to draw a detailed picture of what the ideal house would look like. I'm not the best artist, but if I focus I can create a decent sketch. After drawing a picture of a modern three level home with a wraparound balcony and steeple points, I hung it on my vision board, so I could gaze at it daily. Months later, I found a new apartment. It was nice but looked nothing like the one I envisioned. But, this wasn't a concern at the time. I honestly wasn't aware of the influence this sketch would eventually have since it was created to past time, just for fun. I lived there for about eight months before moving again. Fortunately, a lot of my belongings were still packed, including my vision board. Once again I was on the hunt. I set out scouting neighborhoods and viewing properties. On the way to an open house one day, I drove past this amazing home! I literally slammed on my breaks to catch a better view as I flew by. Lo and behold, a "for rent" sign was posted. I immediately u-turned to inquire. Something about this house was special and from that moment I knew it was the one. Everything in the universe was conspiring favorably. The space was awesome, the location was cool and most importantly, the price was right! I was delighted to become its newest tenant and moved in immediately. Eager to settle in, I committed to unpacking all of my belongings, unlike my previous apartment which was partially filled with boxes and storages bends. As I unpacked the box filled with my office equipment and supplies, I came across my vision board. I chuckled while looking at my hopes and dreams posted to a cork board as if it were childish. Then, I noticed the sketch that was drawn the year prior. I was shocked. In fact, I almost forgot about the drawing since it was out of sight for a while. I couldn't believe what I was seeing. The house that I moved into was almost identical to my sketch. I lived in a huge Victorian style home with Steeple pointes and a balcony that wrapped halfway around the house. All I could do was smile, give praise and be thankful.

2. Visualize it: Imagine your vision. See the end result in your mind exactly as you would like to experience it in reality.

3. Empower and energize: Support the vision with positive emotions or the feeling you would have after acquiring the thing you desire. Charge this thought with good intentions and purpose.
4. Believe: Trust that it shall come to pass, speak in present tense as though it already exists and in time it will be yours. Remove phrases such as "I hope," "I wish" or "I want." Replace such statements with "I am" or "I have." For example, if one desired an immense amount of cash or a loving family, a good present tense affirmative statement would be: "I am extremely abundant and wealthy" or "I am grateful for all that I have and all that is available," "I have a loving and caring family" or "I am grateful for my loving spouse."

    NOTE: Imagining that your desire has already been fulfilled is a very important part of the manifestation process as well as giving gratitude.
5. Give gratitude: Affirm your gratitude daily by giving thanks for all that you have and for the manifestation of your request (though it has not yet materialized.) Begin feeling the emotions that you would feel had it been present.
6. Let go: Upon asking and believing that your desire shall be fulfilled, remain calm and patient with positive expectations that it shall come to pass. Refrain from being annoyed if it doesn't happen in the time frame in which you think it should.

People love instant gratification and often want what they want, when they want it. This can imply a lack of trust and faith in your ability to manifest it, so, please consider the desires of your heart.

7. Allow it to materialize: Was Rome built over night? Or the Pyramids in a day? When the idea or request is made known, know that it may take time. Greatness is a process; manifestation from the intangible (spiritual) realm into physical matter requires order, which is a collective process. Success or anything worth having, for that matter is worth waiting for.

Once you've asked, continue giving gratitude until it materializes and avoid asking for the same thing over again. Many make this mistake. Repetitive requests may imply that one lacks faith in the Universes' ability to produce. Instead, give thanks daily for what you currently have and for those things to come as though they already exist. God created a universe that operates in order and hears all things, good and bad, and is not a favor of persons, so be mindful of what you ask for!

For example, one's request could be: "I'd like to have a new car." Surely you should envision this daily. Upon asking, give thanks for the new car or whatever requests you may have, from that point on:

Inspiration × Motivation + Dedication = Your Destination

"I am extremely great for my means of transportation and my new car as well."

Affirming statements can build your belief and are displayed acts of faith. It is helpful to recite these out loud daily. Your expectations and actions should be on one accord, aligned with your core principals and the infinite "you" that you're becoming.

Ask, believe, and receive.

Things that Do the Mind, Body and Soul Some Good: Affirming Quotes

- "Finish whatever you begin" – Mirror
- "A quitter never wins and a winner never quits" – Napoleon Hill (Think and Grow Rich)
- "Dare to know: enlightenment's motto" – A.C. Grayling
- "Say it–without saying it" – Jack Daniels
- "Energy flows where attention goes" - The Secret
- "Loyalty has no expiration date" – Delta
- "Smile through the tears and you'll awaken from long trials" – Sylvia Brownes
- Ask an it will be given, seek and you will find, knock and the door will be opened for you" – Matthew 7:7
- "Giving is a gateway to glory" – Mirror
- "Fear is the offspring of ignorance" – A.C. Grayling
- "You made me, all the delicate inner parts of my body and knit me together in my mother's womb. Thank you for making me so wonderfully complex! Your workmanship is marvelous- how well I know it. You watched me as I was woven together in the darkness of the womb. You saw me before I was borne. Every day of my life recorded in your book. Every moment was laid out before a single day had passed. How precious are your thoughts

of me- Oh God! They cannot be numbered! I can't even count them; they outnumber the grains of sand! And when I wake up–you are still with me." - Psalm 139: 13-18

- What doesn't kill you–makes you stronger."
- Light exposes the true character of everything"
- "I have set the Lord always before me because he is at my right hand–I shall not be moved" – Psalm 16:8

Chapter VI

(Potential + Faith) - (Fear + Doubt) = Success

(Potential + Faith) - (Fear + Doubt) = Success

One and a Possible

All I need is one and a possible
For me to conquer the world
The next generation's heart throb
I'm humble, not a snob
Accomplished with ease
Life is good, like a cool breeze
Sitting, committing to my goals
Beside me are bountiful trees
Lime green and purple leaves
Providing oxygen to breathe
Thank you, God. I believe
In fact, I know
My love and life are devoted
As I become greater, I'm promoted
I will help and give
I will learn to truly live
If I didn't love or loved to hate
We would quarrel and debate
Truth be told, I love to love
I love to kiss; I love to hug
I love a good cuddle – spooning while we snuggle
I love rainy days and splashing in puddles
I love the simple things:
Like the board game, Life and Trouble

You know,
Things that children like…

One and a possible represent an individual plus potential.
"With God, all things are possible."
Matthew 19:26

"Two are better than one;
They have good reward for their labor
If either of them falls down, one can help the other up."
Ecclesiastes 4: 9-10

(Potential + Faith) - (Fear + Doubt) = Success

The Air that I Breath

Strong, gusting, brisk and swift
Shifting shrubs and bushes
Sifting through rubbish
One man's trash is another's gold
Old and worn, ripped and torn.
Your screeching sneers and whips
Move chimes and blow horns
At times you're warm and gentle
Light and simple
Breezing through my hair
Swaying silk that I wear
Going with obedience onto your destination
Where are you from and where do you go?
So free and clear
I dream to witness you
I try
I sit and ponder, waiting to see your face
Yet you breeze past me without a trace
Upon your return
I give praise and thanks
I feel you, therefore I know you
Vital you are
Required indeed
Air through my lungs I breathe
Often unappreciated

Yet expected
Your significance is cherished
My existence depends upon you
Forbid that I'm ever deprived of you
Despite it all
You take no days off
How honorable!

(Potential + Faith) - (Fear + Doubt) = Success

Journal Entry

It comes to a point in time where one decides to actually live as opposed to merely existing. Often, life can feel as if it's pushing and pulling us around. Perhaps we have not cooperated with the universal principles that govern us. For example, should one think that he or she is able to defy the law of gravity without reaping the consequences, whether good or bad? The solution is within identifying our core beliefs, then learning to align the corresponding values. I finally understand why folks compare life to a game. It is very similar to one learning the rules and functions of a game; we play to have fun and play to win. Learn the rules and functions of life; live a victorious life filled with joy. Learn. Practice. Teach.

My experience has revealed that most people are inclined to operate within their five senses; in other words, what they can see, feel, smell, touch and hear. Humans are intricately constructed creatures; we have an immense amount of potential to be explored and manifested. I measure each area of my life and evaluate my level of satisfaction with current events and circumstances. I ask myself: "Am I happy with the way things are and is it in alignment with my desired vision?

Am I truly and effectively putting to use the resources available to me?"

I Ponder.

Attention goes where energy flows
So, dwell where the kites play and the stars stay
Above cloud nine
High altitude from flower buds and grapevines
Life is good. And though things may fluctuate and the crooked path that once seemed straight
Is responsible for that leap of faith
And is the reason I aspire to be great
It is the ridged uncertainty that keeps me alive.
Therefore, faith is my fuel; love is my foundation.
And I am grateful for every experience;
Life serves as a teacher
And I am life's student.
Honor and obedience is a delightful treat
Haughtiness leads to defeat
So, I listen as life speaks

That voice, it is subtle and sweet
Its gentle whisper sounds familiar
And guiding me is its pleasure

I trust in this guide, as it is my armor
Resting in the bosom of the universe
Free of worry, free of discord.

(Potential + Faith) - (Fear + Doubt) = Success

History / Her-Story

On a journey you've sent me
Placing desires in my heart
Separating me from the masses and the foolish bastards
Who thought it was a race
No! It's a marathon
From dusk 'til dawn
I keep my source before me
Giving praise and glory
Listen clearly
Here's my story:
Young girl
Brooklyn-born
Innocent sweetness; curiosity in full capacity
Living life and loving wrong
Abused emotions
Turned into a woman scorned
Ripped and torn to rebuilt and renewed
Brainwashed and cleansed of incorrect views
Perspectives redirected into a brighter light
I will practice until perfected
And I'm demanding to be respected
Giving thanks and love with all my might
And whether wrong or right
I'm determined to find the best way

A Poet's Journey: Bon Voyage

I work as hard as I play
Live life to the fullest
And I enjoy each and everyday
…That's Her story.

(Potential + Faith) - (Fear + Doubt) = Success

Kat

"Hope is more powerful than a hurricane"
Did hope stop the rain?
Heavily yet heavenly dispensed rain: a monsoon
Pours down; saturates the town; with bloody water it's consumed
Affecting all as it spares little mercy on the young or the old
Catastrophic and compassionless. Kat abducting lost souls
Did she spare those of great faith with the internal burn and a desire to live?
New life she shall give
A cleansing, a fresh beginning
Despite the turmoil that she brings
Blessings are disguised in all things
Deep beneath the apparent surface like buried treasure
Although, from these things we receive no pleasure
Strong faith allow us to move on
"The darkest hour at night is right before the dawn."

Beholding her purge as the waters calm and the winds have ceased
Destruction has settled as Mother Nature is at ease.

A Poet's Journey: Bon Voyage

She looks around and blows cool breeze
Humbled by her presence
The town begins to rebuild and is redeemed.

Chapter VII

Knowledge + Experience = Wisdom

Knowledge + Experience = Wisdom

Metamorphosis

If my air supply was to no longer exist
I'd close my eyes and make a wish
A wish for fins and gills
And more skills
I'd swim to my destination
God forbid there was a shortage of water
I'd head straight for the shore
And become one with the sand
A multitude of me would nurture the land
Going forward with a plan
And then, off to my destination
Morphing into a new creation
I'd become one with the earth;
Embedded like the dirt
I'd go deep like the roots of a tree
I am knowledge. Therefore, I sprout free while faith grounds me
My branches touch the heavens, reaching my destination.
If my wood were to burn and turn into fire
I'd trust in my supplier
Rising above like smoke
My ash would land on Everest's top
Merging with the rock
The peak is my destination
Heaven forbid my mountain be moved

A Poet's Journey: Bon Voyage

Or crumbled into the sea
Wisdom has prepared me to morph unlimitedly
Your grace would rebuild me
And carry me to my destination

Knowledge + Experience = Wisdom

The Cultivated Mind

I recently learned that if you expand your mind
You expand your life.
Growth and inspiration are such delights
I'm grateful for a formal introduction
To a universe I already know
Rekindling the inner light
That now has the opportunity to glow
Glow bright if you will
Be my guide; be my map
For your direction was yearned
Highly needed; in fact
My thoughts are renewed;
I pray my steps follow
I am abundant
Indeed, infinite light shines through
Enabling the world to see
A kinder, wiser version of me
The version that gives their gifts
Without holding back
The one who walks in love
And doesn't look back…
This code is written into my soul
Embedded in my bones

Because love heals
Love makes me whole

Knowledge + Experience = Wisdom

The Woods

My neighborhood was like the woods
I grew up burning Backwoods
While my bros were hooded up in the hood
Hunting for goods
In any neighborhood
Anywhere, any day
If they could, they would
Take a chance
Steal opportunity
All black everything
They wear courage with truth strapped to their waists
A shield of faith
And righteousness as their breastplate
Fearful of nothing
Believing in something
Not falling for anything.
They understand that one must "know thyself"
In order to truly live the good life.
Ask "why" when things don't seem right.
They understand.
To succeed is to try and fail, try and fail
Until you prevail
They get it because every day they live it
Tempted to stray, but they stay

To create a legacy while tilling the land
Bucket in the left, shovel in the right hand
Building castles and carrying out plans
In the woods. We will. We can.

Knowledge + Experience = Wisdom

Think & Drink

I sit
I think
I drink
Reflecting on life's virtues
Dwelling on life's woes
I sip, sip, slow
I think some more
I drink some more
As I yearn for what's within arm's reach
Yet to be grasped
How do I acquire such possessions?
Find a person of pure complement?
And self-satisfaction?
I ponder as I drink
I think and drink.

Infinity

I don't do normal things one would expect me to
I take my time
I stop to smell the roses as if life were a walk in the park.
As if I were outside of space and time.
Walking freely without bounds in an abstract world that infinitely spins
Whose sun arose in the beginning and whose sets have no end?
Infinitely infinite unlike the finite being that grows.
Whose enumerable days gracefully show?
I'm not ordinary. Perhaps extraordinary?
Perhaps I'm like a diamond in the rough
Rigid and tough, formed under pressure.
But I stand above the mantel
Formed under pressure, inevitably evolving into something precious

I don't do things one would expect me to
A derivative of divinity
Outside of space and time
I am infinity.

Knowledge + Experience = Wisdom

Sip Slowly

Cheating? Who's cheating?
Who's lying? Who's doing it?
When are they doing it?
If you defeat the purpose, then why do it?
Blinds open, blinds closed
Tell me. What do you see?
I'm not mad, nor jealous
God sees all things
All the women, all the men
He hears the upbeat love songs that they sing

It starts with a cup of coffee
A conversation
Sip, sip, slowly
… That's when you tell it all to me
You haven't had me but you want me
Brand new to us; hot and fresh
You haven't had me yet
But you're curious
Therefore, I fill your cup
Sip slowly
It goes down fast, once you've had me
I'll refill your cup. Surely, you'll want more of me
And now you're hooked, a few cups was all it took

Damn!
I should've kept it at one cup of coffee
Sip, sip, slowly.

Chapter VIII

Divide and Conquer

Divide and Conquer

Are You...

Simple, sophisticated; sassy, classy
Abundant, happy
Rude, crude; perhaps a shrewd
Are you pessimistic, ridiculous; vindictive and manipulative?
Are you content?
Relaxed, laid back and free
Are you assertive or passive-aggressive?
Rejected, accepted
Suppressed, oppressed, or depressed?
Are you spiritually uplifted or shy?
Perhaps on a natural "high"
Curious, furious;
Inferior, liberated
Concentrated and potent
Perhaps you're the antidote; the potion
Are you the problem or the solution?
Are you...
Confused, in denial, in doubt
Or in love, infused?
Are you ignited – excited or delighted?
How about frightened?
Are you protected or unprotected
Infectious or contagious

A Poet's Journey: Bon Voyage

Are you bold and courageous?
Who are you?
What are you?

Divide and Conquer

Goldie Locks

I wish I may, with all my might
Give a gift with every word I write
It was said by a wise man with locks as long as Goldie's
A broad back, firm grip, a slight limp in his hip
He walked with confidence and when he saw my light
He spoke upliftingly
He said that my future is bright
I trusted in his words, for his tongue had power
I then soaked in and showered
In his blessings and prophecies
"The greatest of them all you are," he said
"Mirror, Mirror, you are a star
Envision your presence affecting those near and far.
When I look into your eyes I see beauty
Your reflection speaks of truth
And truly
It reveals what's underneath
Beyond the flesh–soul deep
Harness this power!"
I smile and sighed; Feeling relieved, I replied:
"I'll make my way,"
Grateful for the spiritual quenching.

My destiny is now clear to me
"I promise, I'll ride the wave."

I focus; I aim.

Liar, Liar

Liar, liar
Pants on fire
The boy who cried wolf
Knew nothing of what it took
To be a man of truth
Instead, he told deceptive stories
Basking in his own glory
Soaking in a shallow pond
As he preys on his next victim
A social parasite is what I was told to call him
Aiming to drain the lives of those who truly live
A taker who takes but does not give
In higher vibrations; truth is innate
A force in which one cannot hide nor escape
It is written, "The truth shall set you free,"
For those who believe.
Pick battles wisely, put up a worthy fight
For every lie I ever told
My spirit tried to digest; but could not
I confess.

Too Much is Not Enough

Enough of the pop culture fluff
The unicorns, rainbows and candy-coated stuff
The allure of bad media ruffles my feathers
It distorts the weather
And the Earth's layers
It's disturbing every leaf on every tree
It's corrupting seeds
Stirring seas
Like cups of tea
"Be free!"
It's written on the walls
The journey has called
Listen.
Gravity inevitably pulls us towards the ground
In this world, up is down
Squares are round
And smiles can quickly turn into frowns
Please, do not be deceived.
Enough is enough
I'm tired of the botched pop culture fluff,
You know, the entertainment that lacks substance
But you still can't get enough
I know, it's tough
Because it's addicting, and simultaneous it's stripping
Every mineral and every stone

Divide and Conquer

Sucking life from every bone
And knowing this, we still can't give it up?
They love to depict quarrels and deception
Feeding off of those misdirected
They inundate us with information and call it culture
So, guard your gateways from virtual vultures

Supermarket

On the way to the market one day
I realized that I needed a new grocery list
All things that I customarily bought, could no longer satisfy my fix
I crave new things; my sweet tooth no longer exists
Dairy that I've purchased, is urban myth
… Who lied and why did they say milk does the body good…
Dairy causes cysts
Those candies, cookies, cakes,
Debbies and Drakes… lead to obesity
Obesity is a catalyst of diabetes
Cute in the face, thick in the waist- no thanks!
And what a waste, those fun un-friendly snacks have become
When I see them, I run!
Cold sweats and shivers
Goose bumps and quivers.
I'm afraid of a sudden relapse
Afraid of the addiction to BHT and the high-fructose corn syrup
That was poured into my cup
Which sucks
Because those witty sophisticated scientists' experiments are detriment

Divide and Conquer

Surely they made it to Santa's naughty list
If such a thing exist
The belief has disappeared like stripes on candy canes
How well-disguised in innocents
Dipped in artificial mint
Extracted from sugarcane;
Converted into an isolated substance

I no longer desire the things I once did
The fruit of the earth is my new fix
What you put in, is what you will get
A wise man said that a healthy grocery list
Consists
Of the foods along the perimeter, outside of the aisles
The leafy whole foods that make your body smile

According to the CDC, more than one-third of American adults are overweight. Many of the products in our markets contain synthetic chemicals that have harmful effects if used over long periods of time. These harmful ingredients deprive the body of the nutrients that it craves. Love yourself. Eat well – live good.

"Health is wealth."

Epilogue

You were born into a world filled with beauty and love, a World that mandates you to learn the rules and regulations that govern it shortly after entering. Like you, the world I call home bears peace and tranquility, as well as turmoil and havoc. I'm on a similar mission as you: growth and progression –the pursuit of purposeful living. Perhaps I have a different ethnic background or geographical location than you, maybe not. Maybe you, too, have experienced some of the joys and hardships of growing up in a fast-paced city, but maybe not.

Such conditions call for an outlet. I chose poetry as mine. Poetry has been the pillar of my self-awareness, personal development and partially responsible for my triumphs. What is your outlet? It is my hope that peace be with you on your pursuit of personal fulfillment and purposeful living. I have much to be grateful for, especially my trials and tribulations. Without them, triumphs would be less gratifying to the soul. Because of them, I've become inspired and determined to live abundantly, love and help others.

Like you, I too have experienced love, joy, pain, anger and rage and know firsthand that remaining hopeful is the first step towards victory. But before I could take the first step, I needed a reason why. "Why" is the driving force that encourages us to pursue and persevere. Your "why" is the reason you get up daily and make a contribution to society. What is your "why"? Is it the family that you love And adore, or maybe the grandparent whose reverent legacy lives on in your heart?

Be that as it may, your "why" should evoke strong emotions. What distinguishes us? Is it belief systems and faith? Is it the application of knowledge or the unique fashion in which God wonderfully constructed each of us? Nonetheless, we are all woven together in the tapestry of life for a divine reason.

I am a helper and defender, here to bring forth good and glorify the kingdom of God. The lessons learned from this journey is to love yourself and others authentically, live purposefully and invest time into knowing thyself. As you continue exploring the endless possibilities of existence, take courage and accept challenges; they will serve you. Allow the infinite intelligence of your subconscience mind to guide you throughout your journey connecting you with the oneness of all that is and will be.

Interactive Workbook

Personal Love List

Now is a great time to create your love list. Use the space below to add all things that you love or love doing. This is a personal inventory that helps identify one's passions and, possibly, hidden talents. Take a few minutes to reflect. For example, I love flowers; I tend to be in a better mood if flowers are in my presence. If you love walks in the park or spending time with family then add it to your list. Remember, feel free to include all hobbies that you enjoy.

- _____
- _____
- _____
- _____
- _____
- _____
- _____
- _____
- _____
- _____
- _____
- _____
- _____
- _____
- _____
- _____

30-Day Challenge

To accept this challenge, you will need to document your daily progress and journal entries. Please feel free to use the space and workbook tools provided. You may also use your personal journal or purchase one, if you do not have one already. In addition, you will need to carve out thirty minutes per day for thirty days.

Though most would agree that it takes about twenty one days to form a habit, recent research disagrees with that theory. This idea suggests that it actually takes about sixty-six days to create a habit. Personally, twenty one days is not enough for me. My victory is usually short-lived once the twenty first day is reached. Something in my mind says that I've reached my goal, so it's okay to stop. I noticed that going beyond the twenty-first day helps further embed the habit until it becomes automated. In my experience, automation usually kicks in around day thirty.

This is a sign that the subconscious is being programmed. Perhaps other factors, such as the complexity of the new habit or how much one actually likes the new habit, contribute to how long it actually takes to form. Habits are routine behaviors that usual go unnoticed and are consistent. I encourage you to adopt healthy habits.

Please note that the thirty minutes allotted daily can be distributed however you choose. Feel free to choose time slots that suit you best and are most appropriate throughout the day. Let's recap what the challenge entails.

First challenge: Take 5 minutes to write a journal entry each day. Your entry should include three things that you are grateful for and one positive experience that occurred throughout the day.

Second challenge: Exercise for 10-15 minutes per day.

Third challenge: Meditate and visualize experiences that you would like to have for 10 minutes each day.

Fourth challenge: Give praise to someone or do a random act of kindness; compliment or help someone each day.

Please use the thirty-day challenge check list on page 110 to track your progress. Simply check off each challenge that was successfully met for the day.

Thirty Day Challenge Check List

	Journal Entry	Physical Exercise	Meditation	Visualization Exercise	Praise or compliment
Day 1					
Day 2					
Day 3					
Day 4					
Day 5					
Day 6					
Day 7					
Day 8					
Day 9					
Day 10					
Day 11					
Day 12					
Day 13					
Day 14					
Day 15					
Day 16					
Day 17					
Day 18					
Day 19					
Day 20					
Day 21					
Day 22					
Day 23					
Day 24					
Day 25					
Day 26					
Day 27					
Day 28					
Day 29					
Day 30					

Journal Entry
Date:

Journal Entry
Date:

Journal Entry
Date:

Journal Entry
Date:

Journal Entry
Date:

Journal Entry
Date:

Journal Entry
Date:

Journal Entry
Date:

Journal Entry
Date:

Journal Entry
Date:

Journal Entry
Date:

Journal Entry
Date:

About the Author

Sam Mirror is the founder of Win-Win Guru, LLC. An organization dedicated to providing personal and professional development resources, life coaching, strategic planning and corporate training. Established in 2016 in the New York Metropolitan area, Sam supports seasoned professionals and young adults alike and has also partnered with PEAK, which is an extension of the School of Health Professions at Long Island University - Brooklyn, to create youth and professional development programs.

Prior to Win-Win Guru's inception, Sam served as a HR Talent Acquisitions professional for a number of prestigious organizations across engineering, finance, health & wellness and non-profit industries and has staffed dozens of multi-million dollar projects. This opportunity stemmed from a decade-long commitment to providing executive support to CEOs of prominent fortune 500 companies and to the Executive Director of the NAACP.

With over 15 years of creative writing experience, Sam Mirror is the recipient of the Martin Luther King Poetry Prize and has authored over 1000 poems. She is passionate about using the creative arts and technology to help people discover their life's purpose and how to fulfill it. Sam's curiosity inspired her to obtain a degree in Information Technology in 2006, and later on a business analyst certification. She is an enthusiastic member of her community and serves as a figure of empowerment.

Sam's philosophy is to think win-win; empowering one to achieve greatness.

www.ingramcontent.com/pod-product-compliance
Lightning Source LLC
Chambersburg PA
CBHW070808230426
43665CB00017B/2535